The Simple Guide to
The Writing Process

 On Demand Instruction

Table of Contents

Introduction

The writing process is a series of steps that writers follow to compose a presentable piece of writing. By incorporating these steps, writers are able to create writing that is clear, organized, and correct. The writing process keeps writers on track and improves the outcome of the writing.

Although the writing process seems simple enough to naturally-organized writers with innate time management skills, for many students and writers the writing process can be overwhelming. In this book, we attempt to present the writing process in a simple, straightforward manner.

Think that the writing process is only for young students? Think again.

Writers between the age of 8 and 108 use the writing process on blogs, articles, stories, reports, research papers, letters, novels, poetry, non-fiction books, and every other imaginable type of writing.

Like all of the books in the Simple Guide Books series, *The Simple Guide to The Writing Process*, is written to the person who may struggle with this topic and the person who needs basic explanations with straightforward examples.

All writers encounter the writing process at some point. A teacher or professor may require student writers to follow the writing process for an assignment. Many professions require workers to write, and the writing process comes in handy, especially with longer pieces like professional reports. As well, novice and professional writers alike follow the writing process to keep themselves and their writing controlled.

The writing process can help a writer get prepared, stay organized, and complete writing tasks on time. Being organized reduces stress and makes the writing process more enjoyable. The writing process is used in the classroom, in the boardroom, and in the community to communicate competently.

Using the writing process in one's writing tasks can mean the difference between a messy, confusing draft and a polished, publishable paper.

The Writing Process

The purpose of writing is to communicate efficiently. Writers take their ideas, thoughts, questions, opinions, and research, and write them so other people can understand them.

People have used writing to communicate their thoughts for thousands of years. One of the benefits of writing is that it is not limited by time. A person can write a play, an essay, or a set of instructions, which may be read 2,000 years later in another country. Because writing allows writers to communicate at any time, readers are also at an advantage since they can read at any time and in any place.

Writing allows people to communicate efficiently, effectively, and exactly. What is impossible to say aloud can be written down. A writer has time and can return to the writing repeatedly to edit and revise until the piece is perfected. Overall, writing improves the communication process for writers and readers.

Where do people commonly write?

Some places where people use writing today are: letters to a government representative to express an opinion, messages to companies to make requests, reports to demonstrate research findings, stories to amuse, and essays to explain how to accomplish complex tasks. As well, emails, texts, and social media posts are all forms of daily writing. Modern society is more dependent on writing than ever before.

How much do we write?

Estimates vary, but some suggest that modern Americans write over 200 pages per year. Imagine that even people who do not consider themselves to be writers can compose so much. If people reflect on all of the emails, texts, letters, and work memos they write each year, the number of pages add up quickly. Since people are writing so much content, the quality of that writing should be considered.

Bearing in mind how much that contemporary people write means that everyone needs the skills to write efficiently. Understanding what the writing process is and being able to use it will make every day writing tasks much easier.

5 Step Writing Process

**The writing process is a series of steps
a writer takes to complete a writing task
from topic to publishable draft.**

1.

Brainstorming
Collect all of the questions, facts, and data on your topic. Complete all necessary research to collect needed information. Hint: Collect twice the facts needed

2.

Planning
Use the information collected in the brainstorm and compile it into an outline or graphic organizer. Hint: Include at least 4 items per paragraph

3.

Drafting
Using the graphic organizer, write the rough draft of the paper. Hint: Even though a perfect paper is not expected in the rough draft, fewer errors in the rough draft mean less editing work

4.

Editing & Revising
Read the rough draft carefully and correct all errors in organization, content, style, and conventions. Hint: This step works best when a writer does through the paper several times.

5.

Presentation
Prepare the paper for presentation, publishing, or assignment submission. Hint: Only perfect writing is acceptable

www.ondemandinstruction.net

What is the writing process?

The writing process is a series of steps that a writer uses to produce a piece of writing. It can be utilized for a short piece of writing like an email, a work memo, or a short answer. But it is more frequently used for longer pieces of writing like essays, research papers, reports, and narratives (stories).

The writing process guides a writer through multiple steps from the very beginning of the process through to an end point, resulting in a perfected piece of writing. Different instructors or academics may suggest using a four, five, six, or seven step process. All of these processes are slightly-altered versions of each other. In this book, the focus is on a five step writing process.

Note

If you run into an instructor, editor, or employer who insists you use certain steps that are different than the ones presented here, follow their suggestions. No system is perfect, but people can sometimes feel dedicated to a particular system.

What are the other steps in the writing process?

In this book, we cover a five step writing process including: brainstorming, planning, drafting, editing/revising, and final drafting. There are different terms used for each of these steps, which will be listed throughout the book to help readers make connections to other books on the writing process.

In the brainstorming step, writers collect many ideas, questions, and research facts around the topic.

In the planning step, writers take the information collected from the brainstorm and organize it into a logical format.

In the drafting step, writers compose the first draft of the essay, paper, or report.

In the editing and revising step, writers correct all errors and make all improvements for the paper.

In the final drafting step, writers perfect their writing and prepare it to share with readers.

Step 1: Brainstorming

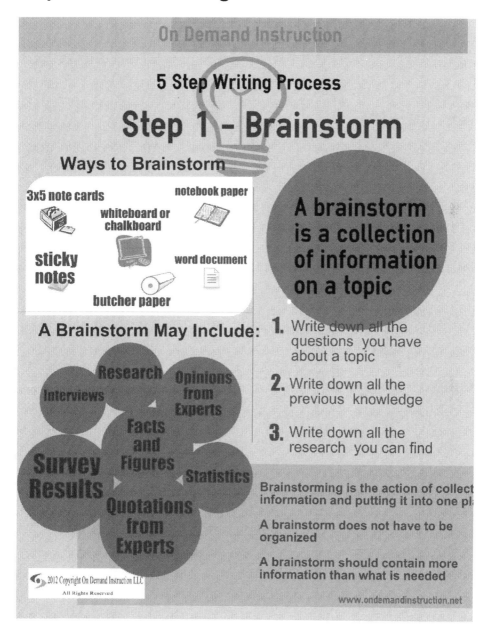

What is it?

In brainstorming, a writer collects all of the information available on the topic. This includes the research a writer does around the topic. Next, the writer jots it down as a brainstorm, which usually looks like a long list.

Why do this?

A writer brainstorms to collect all of the information in one place. That way, writers do not have to go back and look for more information while in the middle of the drafting step. Realizing that one has run short of ideas on page two but needs to submit a five page paper can be daunting, so brainstorming thoroughly at the start can solve this issue before it happens. Always brainstorm more than what is needed.

How does it work?

A writer can assemble a list of all the thoughts, questions, facts, and opinions on the paper's topic. If the expectations include conducting research or referencing expert sources, the research should be done in this step. Errors are unimportant in this step, so just collect ideas, questions, research facts, and thoughts.

What are other terms for brainstorming?

People use different terms to describe the same thing. Writers may run into teachers, editors, or professionals who use any of these terms to describe the brainstorming process. Idea generating, mind mapping, tossing ideas, question collection, group think, or concept mapping.

What are different ways to complete this step?

Use a white board to list ideas, use sticky notes and collect one idea on each, use butcher block paper for a large space, use a recording app or device to amass ideas, or open a document and create a bulleted list.

Tips

Brainstorm more information than will be needed to write the piece. Specifically, try to brainstorm ten items per page. If writing a five page paper, brainstorm 50 items as the first step. Those extra ideas will allow a writer to toss out the less valuable ones and keep just the ideas that work well.

Example Brainstorm

Topic: Explain the importance of eating well

Why eat well	Health benefits	Long term health
Combined with exercise	Diet plans to follow	Fruits-amount?
Meal plans	Macrobiotic diet?	Vegetables-amount?
Snacking benefits	Paleo diet?	Grains-amount?
Water vs. other beverages	Vegan or vegetarian diets?	Proteins-amount?
Alcohol and other drinks	Breakfast, lunch, dinner plans	Fats-types, amounts to avoid?
Fermented foods	Cardio-vascular health	Digestive health

Step 2: Planning

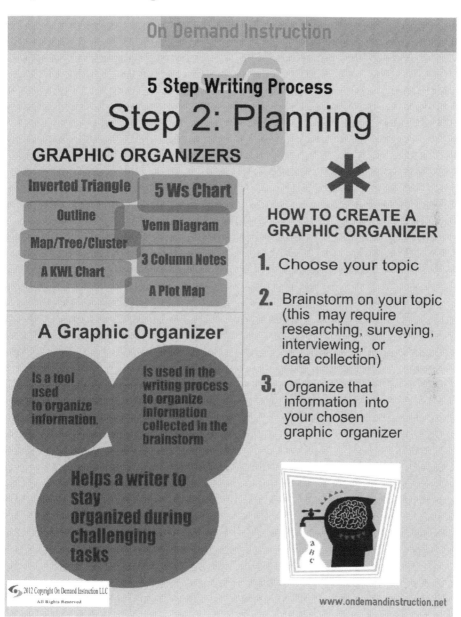

What is it?

Planning is the point where a writer organizes the brainstormed information into a logical sequence. Typically, the writer compiles the information into a graphic organizer or outline.

Why do this?

Organized writing is more enjoyable to write and to read. Using a graphic organizer to plan out one's writing helps the writer to create an organized piece of writing and keeps the writer on task. Graphic organizers are visual tools that can also show where more information is needed.

When a writer attempts to write without a plan, oftentimes the writing is disordered, muddled, and difficult to read. To avoid wasting time, becoming frustrated, and creating poor quality writing, plan out the writing with a graphic organizer.

A graphic organizer is any type of visual device that helps a writer organize information logically. Examples of graphic organizers are: formal outline, informal outline, notecards, mind map, Venn diagram, thematic map, network tree, timeline, pie chart, or story map.

How does it work?

A plan can be completed with a variety of different graphic organizer options: a web or cluster, Venn diagram, formal outline, informal outline, a series of note cards, etc. Writers tend to find one method of planning that they prefer over others. Graphic organizers are visual tools that writers use to organize information.

What are other terms for it?

Other terms for planning are: pre-writing, pre-drafting, outlining, organizing, compiling, and assembling.

What are different ways to complete this step?

Typically, writers take the information from the brainstorm step and organize it into the graphic organizer of choice. That organizer is used to create the rough draft in step 3.

One important factor to consider is that the brainstorm sometimes contains information that is repetitive, off track, or unsupported for the final paper. Because of these reasons, all of the information from the brainstorm will not necessarily be used in the planning. Be ready to discard some of the brainstorm content.

First, reference the writing prompt and expectations before proceeding; this helps to stay on task and not deviate from the writing expectations.

Second, organize the information from the brainstorm into categories. In the example of eating well, a writer might organize the details about food choices into one category and the information about preparing meals into another category.

Next, compile the useful content into groups into the graphic organizer. The content should be visually clear how each of the categories connect to the others.

Tips

During the brainstorming step, it is important to brainstorm more information than is needed for the final paper. Since some information will be discarded, be sure to collect more than you need. It is better to have too much content and discard some than to have too little and need more.

Writers typically use one or two different types of graphic organizers for their writing. In most cases, one style of graphic organizer can be used for most types of writing. By using the same type of organizer over and over, a writer can become more efficient in the writing process.

Although the majority of writing tasks can be planned by using a formal or informal outline, some writers choose different graphic organizers like: web or cluster, Venn diagram, series or note cards, or other tools.

Graphic Organizers

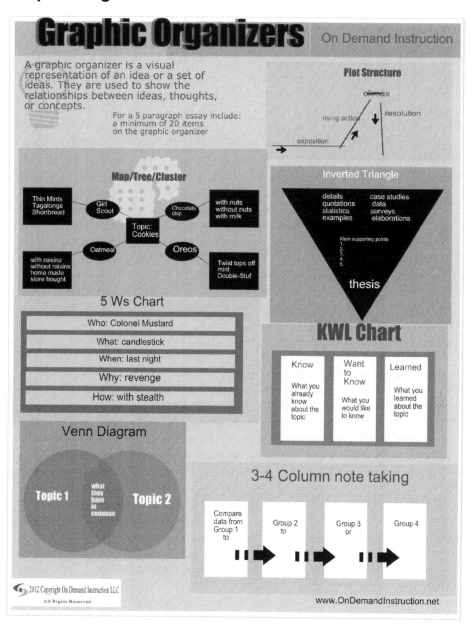

What are graphic organizers?

Graphic organizers are visual tools that writers use in the planning process to organize their information which will be used in the writing process. Graphic organizers keep the writing organized and also keep the writer on track. Since it is very easy to wander off track, using a graphic organizer can help the writer to stick to the topic, which improves the writing quality.

Visual people tend to enjoy graphic organizers that use shapes, colors, and images like: web, cluster, and mind maps.

Kinesthetic people tend to like graphic organizers that allow them to move information around like: note cards and sticky notes. And almost everyone can use an outline to create organized writing.

Example graphic organizer

Topic: Explain the importance of eating well

I.   Health benefits

     a.   Cardiovascular health

     b.   Digestive health

     c.   Long term health benefits

II.   Meal planning

     a.   Breakfast, lunch, dinner

     b.   Snacking

     c.   Water vs. other beverages

III.   Diet Options

     a.   Macrobiotic diet

     b.   Paleo diet

     c.   Vegan or vegetarian diet

Outlines

An outline is a formal type of graphic organizer

Example Outline

I. Topic 1
  A. Main Support 1
  B. Main Support 2
  C. Main Support 3
II. Topic 2
  A. Main Support 1
  B. Main Support 2
  C. Main Support 3
III. Topic 3
  A. Main Support 1
    1. Detail 1
    2. Detail 2
    3. Detail 3
  B. Main Support 2
    1. Detail 1
    2. Detail 2
    3. Detail 3

How to create an outline

Use the information from the brainstorm

Break the information into categories

For each category, create a section of the outline

Fill in the details from the brainstorm until the outline is complete

Organize each category in the outline by categories with: facts, details, support, research, and data

An outline helps a writer stay organized during the writing process.

Outlines improve the writing and the writer

Outlines are used in the writing process to organize information collected in the brainstorm

What are outlines?

Outlines are graphic organizers that writers use to organize the information that will be utilized to create quality writing.

Outlines can be formal with specific patterns using Roman numerals, numbers, and letters in a pattern to show hierarchies. These are used in academic courses and in professional settings.

As well, outlines can be informal with colored fonts, informal numbering systems, and symbols included. These are used for writers but not necessarily submitted for others to view.

Regardless of which graphic organizer style is most attractive to an individual writer, everyone should be able to construct an outline since they are employed so frequently in many settings.

Step 3: Drafting

5 Step Writing Process

Step 3: Drafting

Things to Remember:

WRITING A ROUGH DRAFT

Remember to include your citations

The first draft will be rough

The first draft provides you with the raw material for your essay

1. Start at the beginning and start writing. Use your notes and graphic organizers.

2. Keep writing until you've reached the end of your rough outline. Don't stop or go back to make changes.

Good writing takes time and effort. You can't expect to get it right on the first try. Instead, it's better to write in stages, making improvements with each draft.

What is it?

Drafting is the step where a writer uses the graphic organizer from step 2 to write the first draft of a piece of writing. When writing that first draft, the writer is not usually concerned about spelling, punctuation, and grammar. Instead, the writer is focused on content and organization.

Why do this?

The writing has to start somewhere. Even if the research, brainstorming, and planning take two weeks or two years to complete, eventually the writing needs to begin. The drafting is that starting point of putting words on the page.

Why do this?

What seems to work best for most people is to have their graphic organizer sitting next to them at the computer (in hard copy or on the screen).

While referencing the graphic organizer for content, the writer composes the introductory paragraph. Following along the plan, the writer composes each of the body paragraphs. And finally, the writer composes the conclusive paragraph.

This results in a completed first draft. Even though this draft is unedited and will need ongoing work to be perfected, the first draft is completed.

What are other terms for it?

Other terms for drafting are: rough drafting, scratch writing, and first composition.

What are other ways to complete this step?

Typically, writers will either have a hard copy of their graphic organizers next to the computer while composing the first draft or they will have a split computer screen with the graphic organizer on one screen and the writing draft on the second screen. This allows a writer to glance between the screen and the paper and quickly compose the rough draft.

Tips

Do not attempt to edit and compose at the same time. This is a hazard that lands a lot of writers into trouble. Although some writers may be tempted to try to edit while writing, this practice tends to slow the process significantly, create confusion for the writer, and deflate the writer's enthusiasm for the project. Editing and composing use different parts of the brain and require different processing skills. Do not try and edit while composing.

Another tip is that if writing the introduction paragraph is too difficult, then skip it. Instead, write the body paragraphs first and come back at the end to write the introduction paragraph. Although it may seem counterintuitive to do that, this process can create a much stronger introduction paragraph because the writer knows exactly what the paper will say since it is written first.

As well, it is true that while composing the rough draft writers do not need to be concerned about making mistakes, but it is also true that every mistake made is a mistake to be fixed later on. So, finding a comfortable balance that allows for a speedy composition of the rough draft and also an efficient editing process works out the best for most writers.

Example Draft

Topic: Explain the importance of eating well

Eating well is on the minds of most people today. Living a fast-paced lifestyle and eating processed foods means that many adults suffer from poor eating habits which results in poor health. By eating well, people can reclaim their health and improve their personal lives.

The health benefits of eating well cannot be understated. Heart disease and cancer are the biggest killers, but the risks of both can be diminished by eating well. Cardiovascular and digestive health are improved with a diet rich in vegetables, fruits, and whole grains. The long term benefits of healthy eating are better overall health and better quality of life.

One way to eat well is to plan meals in advance, including a daily plan for breakfast, lunch, and dinner. When people focus on purchasing healthy foods, like fresh vegetables, for planned meals, they tend to snack less and reach for fatty foods less. Water in appropriate quantities completes a daily and weekly meal plan to ensure healthy eating choices.

Every year, dozens of new diets are introduced to the general public, promising to solve people's health issues. By following a doctor-recommended diet that works for each person individually, the best dietary balance can be achieved. Different doctors will recommend a variety of diets including: macrobiotic, paleo, and vegan or vegetarian diets. Each of these vary in their abilities to ensure healthy eating.

Step 4: Editing and Revising

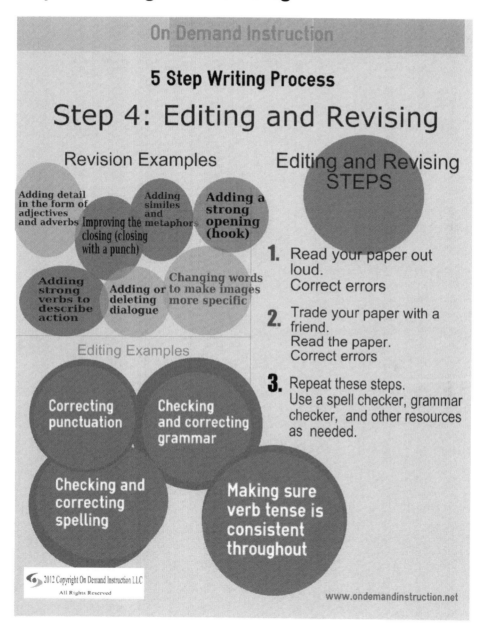

On Demand Instruction

5 Step Writing Process

Step 4: Editing and Revising

Revision Examples

Editing and Revising STEPS

Adding detail in the form of adjectives and adverbs

Improving the closing (closing with a punch)

Adding similes and metaphors

Adding a strong opening (hook)

Adding strong verbs to describe action

Adding or deleting dialogue

Changing words to make images more specific

1. Read your paper out loud. Correct errors

2. Trade your paper with a friend. Read the paper. Correct errors

3. Repeat these steps. Use a spell checker, grammar checker, and other resources as needed.

Editing Examples

Correcting punctuation

Checking and correcting grammar

Checking and correcting spelling

Making sure verb tense is consistent throughout

www.ondemandinstruction.net

What is it?

Editing and revising is the step where the writer locates and corrects the errors in the rough draft. A writer reads over the piece of writing several times and corrects errors.

Look for these:

Spelling

Punctuation

Grammar

Organization

Content

Style

Professionalism

Meeting the task's expectations

Appropriately addressing the audience

Why do this?

Every writer makes mistakes that must be corrected. Most novelists have to rewrite their books several times to get them just right. This is a normal part of the writing process. Assuming that a rough draft is perfect without any editing or revising is unrealistic. Since composing and editing use different parts of the brain and diverse abilities, a writer needs to use completely different skills to edit and revise the writing.

How does this work?

Once step 3 is completed and the rough draft is finished, the editing and revising can begin. Typically, a writer will read through the piece of writing several times to locate and correct errors. Some writers will read through the paper once to locate errors and will revise the paper in the second part of the step. Correct and edit simultaneously or separate them into two tasks if desired. The only difference is personal preference.

What are other terms for it?

Other terms for editing and revising are: correcting, reviewing, or rewriting.

What are different ways to complete this step?

First, read through the paper silently and correct all errors. Then read it out loud to oneself and correct the errors. Next, read the piece out loud to another person and ask them to indicate when the writing does not make sense or needs improvements. When reading a paper out loud, different errors will appear than when reading silently. Last, trade papers with another person and edit for each other. It is oftentimes easier to locate other people's writing errors than one's own.

Another method to use when editing a paper is to read it and edit for one issue at a time. Use the checklist on the following page as a guide to locating errors to revise. For writers who find holistic editing challenging, this method can be more successful.

Tips

Use a checklist to edit and revise. Checklists can make this step much more efficient and detailed.

Infographic: Grammar Rules

On Demand Instruction

GRAMMAR

Grammar teaches the correct forms of written and spoken language.

When grammar is ignored or abused, sentences do not make sense and meanings get lost.

Grammar is why Yoda talks funny or how we can distinguish the meaning of "cat eats mouse" from "mouse eats cat."

Syntax
How the parts of a sentence go together.

Semantics
The meanings of words, sentences, phrases, or text.

Phonetics
The sounds of speech and how they're made, how they combine to make words, and the written symbols that represent them.

Morphology
The forms and formations of words in a language.

www.OnDemandInstruction.net

Infographic: Punctuation Rules

Punctuation Rules

End punctuation

period, exclamation point, question mark

- Use a period at the end of a statement.
  Ex. I finished reading the book.

! Use an exclamation point after a statement
  that expresses strong emotion.
  Ex. I never said that!

? Use a question mark at the end of a direct
  question.
  Ex. What did he say to you?

Apostrophe

Use to form a possessive noun.
Ex. Brittany's birthday party
is on Saturday.

To show missing letters.
Ex. I can't [cannot] think of
a time when I didn't
[did not] cry at this
movie.

Quotation marks

" "

Used to set off a piece of
dialogue.
Ex. "I would like an apple,"
Shannon said.

Comma

Use a comma before a coordinator
(for, and, nor, but, or, yet, so) that
links 2 main clauses.
Ex. I never said that, but he
thinks I did.

To separate items.
Ex. I want a pony, dolls, lipstick,
and a purse for my birthday.

After an introductory word group.
Ex. When your ship comes
in, be ready to sail.

In pairs to set off interruptions.
Ex. She, of course, said
that she didn't want to go.

Semicolon, colon, dash

; A semicolon coordinates two
main clauses.
Ex. He isn't interested at all;
he is actually the opposite.

: Use a colon to set off a series after
a complete main clause.
Ex. It is time for Christmas: pine
trees, trimmings, turkey, and
family are on their way.

— Use a dash to emphasize a short
summary after a complete main
clause.
Ex. The final gift lay at the bottom
of Pandora's box- hope.

Infographic: Spelling Rules

Spelling Rules

Use I before E except after C or when the sound is A like in neighbor and weigh.

Examples: chief, belief, grief, piece

Some exceptions: weird, ancient, foreign

Drop the final E in a word before a suffix beginning with a vowel.

Examples: slide + ing = sliding
hope + ed = hoped
bike + er = biker

Some exceptions: noticeable, truly

Change a final I to Y before a suffix, unless the suffix starts with I.

Examples: party + ies = parties
try + ing = trying
copy + ier = copier

Some exceptions: memorize, journeying

Double a final single consonant before a suffix beginning with a vowel when
1. a single vowel comes before the consonant
2. the consonant ends an accented syllable or a single-syllable word

Examples: stop + ing = stopping
stoop + ed = stooped
delight + ful = delightful

Spell checkers

Spell checkers can be useful, but don't rely on them. They will not catch words that sound the same such as their and they're or your and you're.

Adding prefixes

Adding a prefix does not usually change the spelling of a word.

Examples: misspell
dissatisfied
unnecessary

Keep working on it!

Keep a dictionary handy. Pay attention to how words are spelled when you are reading. Keep a list of words you know you have trouble with.

www.OnDemandInstruction.net

Editing Checklist

Use this editing checklist when editing and revising a paper.

Were the task's directions followed exactly?

Is every word correctly spelled?

Is all of the paper's punctuation correct?

Is all of the grammar properly used?

Is one verb tense used?

Is one point of view used?

Is the appropriate tone, voice, and style used?

Has the audience been appropriately addressed?

Is it organized (introduction, body, conclusion)?

Is the information interesting, timely, valid, and supported?

Is the piece presented academically and professionally?

Have the task's expectations been met or exceeded?

Step 5: Presentation

5 Step Writing Process

Step 5: Final Drafting Publishing or Presentation

The Importance of Proofreading

Do not underestimate the importance of going over your work and looking for errors. Spell check, though useful, is not a replacement for proofreading. It does not catch words that are spelled correctly but used incorrectly, nor grammatical errors. Having someone else read your paper can help too.

The Final Draft

Things to Keep in Mind

Care about what you are writing

Use your own words, except when you are directly quoting

Cite all of your references in the proper format

Check and double check your facts

Write first, edit later

1. The final draft is the completed paper you will hand in.

2. By this point, your paper should be pretty polished. Sentences should flow smoothly and there should be no errors in the paper.

Checklist before you turn your paper in:

Content
assignment is complete
information is appropriate

Organization
the order of the information is logical

the introduction and conclusion are clear & related

Style
style and tone are appropriate
sentences are smooth and efficient
the paper is error free

Format
the assignment is in the required format

www.ondemandinstruction.net

What is it?

This is the final draft that will be submitted, shared, or published. You want to rewrite the paper to make it 100% perfect.

Why do this?

Writers want to present their best work in any writing, whether they are drafting a letter, an essay, or a full-length book. The quality of one's writing is a reflection of who and what each person is. When a writer submits sloppy writing for review, that writer appears to be sloppy. So, sharing well-polished writing is important.

How does this work?

Sit down with the edited draft of the paper and write it perfectly. Correct all errors, verify it, read it out loud, check the heading, spacing, and other formatting areas. It should be 100% perfect when submitted.

What are other terms for it?

Other terms for final drafting are: publishing, submitting, sharing, presenting, or polishing.

What are different ways to complete this step?

In this step, the writer has already edited and revised the rough draft, which may have included several rewrites of the original copy. Now, the writer is checking and verifying before sharing the piece with other people.

The best way for most writers to complete this step is to trade papers with another writer. Since locating our own errors is quite challenging, working with a peer to polish the final draft can be a positive experience. Since the majority of the errors should already be revised and corrected, this step should not require a significant amount of time.

Presentation Checklist

Use this final checklist when polishing a final draft.

Are the assignment's directions followed exactly?

Were all errors from step 4 corrected?

Check page, font, and margins formatting.

Check works cited, bibliography, in-text citations, and end notes for format per research guide book's specification (i.e. MLA, APA).

Are all references properly cited and included?

Do a plagiarism check.

Does anything else accompany the paper (title page, letter of inquiry, references, etc.)?

Is this paper a reflection of your best work?

Infographic: Writing Styles

Writing Styles

Different Types of Writing Require Different Styles

Persuasive

Persuasive writing is used in situations where the writer wants to convince the reader into agreement.

Examples: advertising, marketing materials, movie trailers, and political speeches or writing.

Expository

Expository writing is where the writer is explaining something to the reader. This may include: informational materials, brochures, websites, and essays. Included in expository writing would be: research papers, health pamphlets, and instructional materials like user's manuals.

Narrative

A narrative is a story. It may be presented as a poem, short story, or dramatic piece. Overall, it is a situation where the writer is telling a story of conflict and its resolution.

Compare/Contrast

Writing that shows how two or more things are either similar or different is comparison/contrast. Typically, a writer will want to stick with either comparison OR contrast not both.

Examples: charts that show product differences, travel brochures that give a list of similar activities in an area, and political materials that show the differences between candidates are all comparison/contrast style.

Research

Research writing is any writing that depends upon researched information from experts to support the thesis statement.

Research can be the most reliable style of writing because the writer is distanced from the topic. The content comes from the researched data, statistics, quotations, and examples from topic experts.

OnDemandInstruction.net

Writing Process Examples

Many writers enjoy seeing examples when learning about the writing process. Seeing is believing so watching the writing process in action can change the learning experience for many writers, especially novice writers. In this section, we include the full writing process from brainstorm all the way through final draft for six different writing tasks:

Short answer/short response

Expository essay

Persuasive letter

Professional memo

Research response

Use these examples as a means for not only seeing how the writing process can be put into use but also learning how to follow these steps for your writing tasks.

Infographic: Different Writing Styles

On Demand Instruction

Different Writing Styles

Writing can seem intimidating. In fact, it can actually be quite simple if you approach it the right way.

First, you have to know what style of writing you will compose.

Narrative Writing

Tell a story
Real-life experience
Involve the reader
Make it as vivid as possible
Engage the reader
Write in first person
Build toward drawing a conclusion
or making a personal statement

Comparison or Contrast Writing

Show how two things are similar
OR
Show how two things are different
Anecdotes
Comparative data
Shared statistics
Charts and graphs
Survey results
Compare professional opinions

Expository Writing

Informative
Gives just the facts
Present a balanced analysis
Explain or define a topic
Use facts, statistics, and examples
Basis in fact, not opinion or emotion
Don't write in first person
Can be many types of essay, such as compare/contrast, cause/effect, or how-to

Persuasive Writing

Convince the reader to accept your point of view
Build a case using facts and logic
Give examples, expert opinion, and sound reasoning
Present all sides of the argument
Communicate clearly without doubt or question why their position is correct

www.OnDemandInstruction.net

Short Answer Example

A short answer or short response is the same type of writing under two terms. It is typically a one to three paragraph response that fully answers the writing prompt. The writing prompt could be a question that needs an answer (sent via email, asked in person or written in a letter) or a reading response task on an exam. People use short answers in a wide variety of roles—in school, at work, and when interacting with friends and family such as on email.

For the purposes of this task, the writing prompt will be:

Why have comic book characters grown significantly in popularity in recent years?

For this prompt, we need to follow the entire writing process: brainstorm, organize, draft, edit, and final draft.

Infographic: Short Answers

On Demand Instruction

Short Response

What is a short response?

A short answer response requires the student to answer a specific question, usually in 1-3 paragraphs.

How to compose

Read the prompt all the way through before you answer.

Make sure you understand what it is asking.

Answer all parts of the prompt and follow directions. If it asks multiple questions, be sure to answer them all.

Use a variety of sentence lengths and types.

Use standard English and proofread your work carefully before you turn it in.

Your response should be 1-3 paragraphs, and each paragraph should be at least 5 sentences long.

If you have questions, ask before responding.

www.OnDemandInstruction.net

Short Answer Brainstorm

Original comic books 1930s-1950s	Marvel Comics	DC Comics
Comics as literature?	Avengers	Superman, Batman, Wonder Woman
Rise of interest in pop culture	Ironman, Spiderman, Thor, Black Widow	Portrayals of heroes
Comic Cons and other conventions	Fantastic Four	Fan fiction
Rise in interest in science and science fiction?	Guardians of the Galaxy	Justice League
STEM?	Creativity	Role models

Brainstorm Analysis

The brainstorm above includes 18 items in total. Three of the items are questions. Whenever creating a brainstorm, asking a couple of questions can help to expand ideas and include passing thoughts that might turn into useful details. This brainstorm also includes broad topics like Marvel and DC Comics as well as specific details like Black Widow and Wonder Woman.

This brainstorm is also varied because it contains more than one type of detail. That can be very useful when organizing the content. A writer could use this brainstorm to collect enough ideas that will be used for organizing the draft, or a writer could expand upon one of these details (such as: Comic Cons) to focus on one specific area of this prompt.

Again, the purpose of the brainstorm is to give the writer a mental space to come up with as many ideas, questions, and details around the topic as possible. Writers might include personal examples, past experiences, existing knowledge, questions, facts, details, or anything else related to the topic.

After the brainstorm is thorough enough to move onto the next step, the writer needs to make decisions about its content. In some cases, a writer will use all of the brainstormed items in the paper's draft, although this is rare. In most cases, the writer will discard about 25% of the brainstorm ideas and use the rest in the paper. Occasionally, a writer will focus on just a couple of the brainstormed items and discard the rest.

During the process of organizing, the writer transfers information from the brainstorm into the graphic organizer. The reason for this is to create an organized plan for the ideas, which can be used to draft the writing. If organization is sloppy at this point in the writing, then the writing will be sloppy later on. So, the writer should focus on strong organization once the initial ideas are on paper.

Infographic: Organization

On Demand Instruction
Get Organized

Is Organization Different in Different Types of Writing?

What is Organization?

Organization is the structure of a piece of writing.

In stories or novels, writers can use any kind of organization, though following a plot structure is common; exposition, rising action, climax, falling action, and conclusion.

In essays and research reports, writers will use three types of paragraphs in this order: introduction body conclusion

In multi-media presentations, writers also begin with an introduction, offer support, then conclude on the topic.

Organization

By using clear organization, a writer can:

- Communicate more clearly and effectively
- Stay on topic
- Ensure the writing makes sense

How does a reader know when organization is clear?

- The reader understands what the writer is communicating
- The reader has received information is order
- The writing comes across as making sense, even if the topic is complex

Get organized! Stay organized!

www.ondemandinstruction.net

Short Answer Planning

For this short answer, we use a mind map to create the graphic organizer. This type of tool is useful for visual thinkers who like to see their thoughts laid out with images, shapes, and colors.

The top yellow bubble shows the original prompt. When writers include the prompt, they tend to have an easier time keeping track of information and ensuring that the content connects well to the assigned task. The second yellow bubble down includes the thesis statement: Comics have become the heroic literature of modern day. In every graphic organizer, the writer should state the thesis statement, even if stating it last after all of the details are added.

The light green bubbles make up the broad, general support for the thesis statement. These include: Marvel, DC Comics and Heroes. Marvel and DC Comics are both examples of companies that create comic books and other comic-style art like films, cartoons, and graphic novels. These points support the thesis statement and also open up the discussion for the details to delve deeper into the subject.

The third layer is the darker green, which lays out the details. All the details support the thesis statement and give the reader a more thorough understanding of the thesis and its importance. The details include: Avengers, Guardians of the Galaxy, Fantastic Four, Superman/Supergirl, Justice League, Wonder Woman, pop culture, STEM (science, technology, engineering, and math), and science fiction.

The purpose of any graphic organizer is to organize the brainstormed information into a format that can be used to create the written draft. Notice that some of the brainstormed ideas were not used in the graphic organizer. Writers need to decide which information to use and which to discard. Use the content that logically works together to answer the prompt.

The thesis statement is the most important element of the response, and most writers compose a thesis during the planning stage. When writers review the brainstormed information, they need to categorize the content into a logical pattern. The brainstorm provides information on the topic that leads to an answer of the research question or prompt. The thesis statement is the result of the information brainstormed and collected. It then drives the writing forward by being its purpose.

Typically, a plan should include: the thesis statement and three to five supporting examples for each paragraph. So, if the response is only a paragraph long, a thesis statement and five supporting examples should be sufficient. If the response is three paragraphs long, once the plan contains enough information to get the writer organized, it is time to write the first draft.

Infographic: Short Response

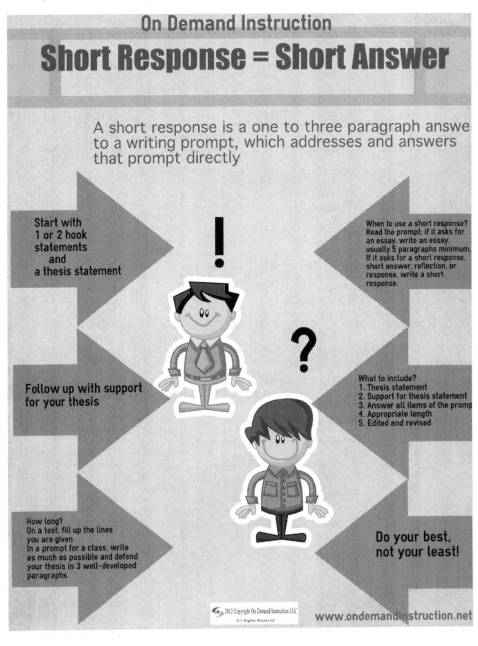

On Demand Instruction

Short Response = Short Answer

A short response is a one to three paragraph answer to a writing prompt, which addresses and answers that prompt directly

Start with
1 or 2 hook
statements
and
a thesis statement

When to use a short response?
Read the prompt; if it asks for
an essay, write an essay,
usually 5 paragraphs minimum.
If it asks for a short response,
short answer, reflection, or
response, write a short
response.

Follow up with support
for your thesis

What to include?
1. Thesis statement
2. Support for thesis statement
3. Answer all items of the prompt
4. Appropriate length
5. Edited and revised

How long?
On a test, fill up the lines
you are given
In a prompt for a class, write
as much as possible and defend
your thesis in 3 well-developed
paragraphs

Do your best,
not your least!

www.ondemandinstruction.net

Short Answer Drafting

Once the writer has enough information organized in the plan, writing the first draft is the next step. The following three paragraphs contain the short answer response to the example prompt.

Example

Have you wondered about the new fascination with comic book characters and their increased popularity? Comics have become the heroic literature of modern day. DC Comics have shared their characters from comic books into films and books.

DC Comics was the first comic book publisher to bring their characters to the big screen. Superman, Supergirl and Wonder Woman all became popular movie and cartoon characters.

Marvel succeeded in engaging audiences with their characters in movies. The Fantastic Four, Guardians of the Galaxy, and Avengers have been featured in multiple movies.

Short Answer Editing and Revising

The writing of this rough draft took about five minutes to create and it includes no editing. So, when looking at this piece, a writer would start editing and revising at the introduction. The introduction paragraph should include: a hook to pull in the reader, the thesis statement and broad, general support for the thesis. An improvement to the rough draft would be to include both Marvel and DC Comics in the examples. The introduction paragraph ends abruptly, so adding a conclusion sentence would make it smoother.

The body paragraphs include useful information but not enough of it. In the first body paragraph, the writer could add an analysis about why DC Comics and their characters are valuable, especially to young readers who tend to gravitate towards comics.

The final paragraph comes across as flat. It contains only two sentences-a topic sentence and a detail sentence about Marvel comics. This one could be improved with additional depth and breadth of information.

After the writer improves the ideas and organization, move through the editing checklist. Verify that the directions were followed, the piece is well presented, and the expectations are met. Then check for errors in: spelling, grammar, mechanics, and usage. Once the editing and revising are finished, the writer should move onto the final drafting step.

Short Answer Presentation

The final writing process step is a quick one compared to the editing and revising, which is typically the longest step. Rewrite the rough draft into a presentable piece. Then run down the Presentation Checklist to verify that the piece is: a high-quality representation of excellent writing, perfected in every way, and properly formatted. The short answer presentation piece follows.

Example

Have you wondered about the new fascination with comic book characters and their increased popularity? Comics have become the heroic literature of modern day. Marvel and DC Comics have shared their characters from comic books into films, books, and pop culture paraphernalia. Because comic book characters are heroic, they heighten the reader's interest in educational areas like science fiction, popular culture, science, and math.

DC Comics was the first comic book publisher to bring their characters to the big screen. Superman, Supergirl and Wonder Woman all became popular movie and cartoon characters. DC Comics began using their comic characters in films, books, and popular culture marketing in the 1970s and continue that tradition today.

Marvel succeeded in engaging audiences with their characters in recent films and continue to release new films every year that exemplify heroism. The Fantastic Four, Guardians of the Galaxy, and the Avengers have been featured in multiple films. Their images adorn t-shirts, backpacks, and every object imaginable. Comic characters have become the modern day heroes, and comic books and films the contemporary version of heroic literature.

Infographic: Improving Your Writing

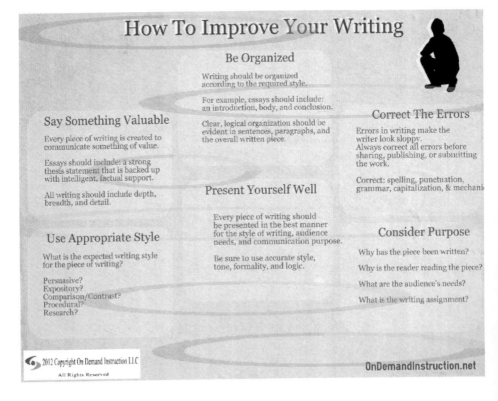

Expository Essay Example

Expository writing is by far the most commonly used forms. Writers use expository writing for business letters, personal emails, essays, blogs, comparison/contrast pieces, and any written communication where something is being explained. Anytime that a writer needs to explain, illustrate, or instruct on a topic, expository writing is the best method to use.

What are some examples of expository writing? A cover letter for a resume is an explanation of one's professional experience and expertise. So is a letter to grandmother. Sending her a letter that explains what the family is up to with updates on the kids and the new dog is another use for expository writing. A brochure that compares three different vehicles to demonstrate the superiority of one of them is another example of expository writing. Technically, research writing such as papers on studies that are published in professional journals are also expository writing. And a professional email with an overview of how a new account should be handled is another form of expository writing.

Expository writing is the most common form that we use. Newspapers, magazines, and other forms of media utilize expository writing to communicate their messages, especially when that message is a factual, journalistic one. Even an article about who a celebrity is dating is a form of expository writing. The writer is explaining factual information, so that is expository.

All journalism falls into expository writing form, although some certainly has a persuasive slant to it. Unfortunately, some journalistic venues choose to persuade the public into believing incorrect, highly politicized, or biased information. Regardless of the ethical level of a journalistic media, the writing form should be expository.

Since expository writing's purpose is to explain, it tends to be highly organized. Anytime that an email, essay, or article is an exposition, it tends to have easily-recognizable introduction, body, and conclusion sections. The writing is rarely artistic in the sense of being abstract in a way that the reader would have a hard time following along. Expository writers want their readers to comprehend easily.

For our purposes of illustration, we will share an expository essay. This will include a brainstorm, plan, rough draft, editing and revising notes, and a final draft for presentation. The prompt for this essay is: Explain which book made the biggest impact on you. We will address the book *My Antonia* by Willa Cather.

Infographic: Expository Writing

Expository Writing

Expository writing has the purpose of explaining a concept. A writer's job with an expository piece is to take a reader from a point of not knowing very much about the topic to a point of understanding the topic very well.

How does a writer explain?

A writer can explain a topic by including:
*Explanation
*Evidence
*Events
*Statistics
*Quotations
*Conclusions from research
& the inclusion of many other forms of factual information to explain and expand upon the topic.

A good expository essay allows a reader to understand the topic completely.

www.OnDemandInstruction.net

Expository Essay Brainstorm

For this brainstorm, we are going to list the free-associated ideas. Some writers prefer a list to a chart or other methods of collecting brainstormed information. Do keep in mind that regardless of what type of writing you are attempting or how long it is, try to brainstorm five to ten ideas per paragraph. So, when writing a five paragraph essay, try and brainstorm about 25-50 ideas. This will allow some of the ideas to be thrown out without limiting the scope of the piece.

Willa Cather-Nebraska writer

Late 19th century setting

Story of pioneers and people homesteading

Immigrants from Bohemia (Czechoslovakia)

Immigrants from Sweden and Norway

Very hard, physical work for everyone

Lack of food

People living in sod house—very cold, cramped, miserable

Jim's story of how he sees Antonia

Antonia's hardships in life

Antonia moved from her country

She loses her father

Her brother is a brute

She works harder than a man at physical labor

She is tricked by her fiancée

Antonia's life is one of hardship and challenge

Jim sees Antonia with a romantic vision

He does not love Antonia romantically but loves the idea of her

Antonia is symbolic of the hardships of the prairie and of homesteading

Jim and Antonia are separated by social class

Jim is from people who moved to town to stop doing manual labor

Antonia is connected to the land and symbolically tied to it

Antonia never completely leaves the land, even though she lives in town as a teenager

Jim leaves the land and moves to the east coast

Jim grows up in town away from the prairie

Jim loses his connection to the prairie and starts his new life

Jim's memories of Antonia are even more romanticized

Antonia's life is not romantic. She is old, unhealthy, poor, and overburdened

By leaving Nebraska, Jim leaves the prairie and hardships and Antonia becomes a vision of the past

Expository Brainstorm Analysis

Sometimes, while creating a brainstorm, ideas will naturally come up in groups. This can be very helpful by making the next step of planning because they are grouped together already. It is very common to follow an idea for several minutes while brainstorming with many details coming up all at once.

Whenever creating a brainstorm, consider asking questions, including thoughts of new information, unanswered questions, and elements that do not make sense. Sometimes, starting with the questions that you do not know can create a great introduction into what you do know.

Just about any information is valid for a brainstorm. Useful pieces to include are: questions, general topics, supporting details, thoughts, statistics or data, and things you wondered about.

In this brainstorm, we have more than 25 ideas, which is very useful. This will allow us to throw out some of these details since we have more than we need. Brainstorming more than is necessary makes the planning and drafting stages more manageable.

Expository Essay Planning

For this piece, we will use an informal outline to plan the essay. All of our information for the outline will come from the brainstorm, and since we have a large brainstorm, the process should be fairly quick. The outline will allow us to create a plan that is highly organized and will show a hierarchal structure between the items. When writing an essay, the more organized the plan is, the more organized the essay will be. So, any steps that writers take in the brainstorming and planning steps will help the drafting step to be smoother.

Expository Example Plan

Thesis Statement: By leaving Nebraska, Jim abandons the prairie and its hardships; his admiration for Antonia grows in that Jim romanticizes her strengths and diminishes her losses.

Support: Jim leaves the Nebraska prairie in a series of steps that separate him from the land. As he separates from the land, he romanticizes it and those associated with it.

Jim moves from the farm to Black Hawk, then to Lincoln, then to New York.

When Jim arrives on the farm, he is already at a higher status than the Bohemian immigrants because his grandparents homesteaded previously.

When Jim moves to Black Hawk, his status increases, as it does when he moves to Lincoln, and then to New York.

Support: Each of Jim's moves take him up the social ladder and his own hardships decrease, while those on the prairie do not necessarily feel this same level of relief.

When Jim leaves the farm for town, his access to fine goods increases as does his associations with people of the merchant and management classes.

When Jim moves to Lincoln, he has a greater access to the fine things in life as does Lena whom he dates briefly. Lena's business prospects increase dramatically as she becomes a sought after seamstress of fine clothing.

Finally, Jim's ultimate move to New York bring him to one of the world's most cosmopolitan cities. With this move comes his fear of returning to Black Hawk and Antonia, as he does not want to see her broken by poverty and deprivation. He wants to keep a romanticized vision of her life as being carefree and happy.

Support: Jim's romantic vision comes true for him at the end of the story.

He and Antonia hold onto the shared, incommunicable truth of their mutual past

Jim has envisioned Antonia's life through a romantic lens as though her continued connection with the prairie brought her youthful vivacity.

Though at the end, Antonia still displays a strong sense of self and pride in her life because she has not changed much from the youthful rebellious young girl, she has experienced poverty and deprivation that comes with living off the land.

Notice that on this plan, the brainstormed information has been expanded and added to. It is perfectly fine to expand on information at any time during the writing process. As well, most of the content from the brainstorm was left off of the plan. Any of the missing details could be added in at a later time if needed. For example, if a paragraph needed more detail, returning to the brainstormed list could produce more content to make a paragraph more robust.

Expository Essay Drafting

As with every stage of the writing process, the more detailed and thorough that a writer can be, the easier the following steps are. So, a thorough outline will make for a quick rough draft. Some instructors will tell writers to think nothing of organization during the early parts of the writing process (brainstorm, plan, and rough drafting), but anyone who ignores organization pays the price in time during the editing and revision stage, and waiting so long to get organized can create unnecessary confusion.

Rough Draft Example

In the novel *My Antonia* by Willa Cather, readers experience what life for immigrants was like as newcomers from Eastern Europe homestead for the first time on the unforgiving Nebraska prairie. Later in the book, some homesteaders leave the connectedness with the prairie by moving to towns and cities, which allows them to move up through the social strata. By leaving Nebraska, the protagonist Jim abandons the prairie and its hardships; his admiration for Antonia grows in that Jim romanticizes her strengths and diminishes her losses. Each step that Jim takes away from the land is a step up the sophisticated social ladder for him. These steps increase Jim's romantic notions of Nebraska and of Antonia. In the end, Jim's vision of a vibrant, unbroken Antonia comes true in some ways.

Jim leaves the Nebraska prairie in a series of steps that separate him from the farms. As he separates from the land, he romanticizes it and those associated with it. Jim moves from the farm to Black Hawk, then to Lincoln, then to New York. When Jim arrives on the farm, he is already at a higher status than the Bohemian immigrants because his grandparents lived homesteaded previously. When Jim moves to Black Hawk, his status increases, as it does when he moves to Lincoln, and then to New York.

Each of Jim's moves take him up the social ladder and his own hardships decrease, while those on the prairie do not necessarily feel this same level of relief. When Jim leaves the farm for town, his access to fine goods increases as does his associations with people of the merchant and management classes. When Jim moves to Lincoln, he has a greater access to the fine things in life as does Lena whom he dates briefly. Lena's business prospects increase dramatically as she becomes a sought after seamstress of fine clothing. Finally, Jim's final move to New York bring him to one of the world's most cosmopolitan cities. With this move comes his fear of returning to Black Hawk and Antonia, as he does not want to see her broken by poverty and deprivation. He wants to keep a romanticized vision of her.

Jim's romantic vision comes true for him at the end of the story. He and Antonia hold onto the shared incommunicable truth of their shared past. Jim has envisioned Antonia's life through a romantic lens as though her continued connection with the prairie brought her youthful vivacity. Though at the end, Antonia still displays a strong sense of self and pride in her life because she has not changed much from the youthful rebellious young girl, she has experienced poverty and deprivation that comes with living off the land.

Expository Editing and Revising

Overall, this is a decent rough draft. It consists of a clear introduction, defined body paragraphs, and a thorough conclusion. Since organization is so important for expository essays, having the organization in place early makes for light work through the editing and revising process.

To improve this essay, start with the introduction, which is only one sentence in the rough draft. Ideally, the introduction should include a hook, thesis statement, three to seven general supporting statements, and a conclusion sentence. The introduction's purpose is to introduce the topic by stating the thesis statement and its general support.

Once the introduction familiarizes the readers in a thorough manner, move into the body paragraphs. The content in these body paragraphs are comprehensive in that each one is focused on a single topic, each one supports the thesis statement, and each provides detailed support.

What these body paragraphs lack are transitions between the paragraphs and between the ideas. Adding transition words and phrases could smooth out that issue. As well, all body paragraphs should begin with an introduction sentence and end with a conclusion sentence. This creates polished paragraphs and improves the overall style.

The rough draft ends with a thud because the conclusion paragraph is missing altogether. A conclusion paragraph should restate the thesis statement and the main support. It should leave readers with a clear vision of what the writer is trying to communicate and should leave the reader satisfied with the new information gained from the piece. Since this draft is missing its conclusion, a thorough conclusion paragraph should be added to the final draft.

Expository Essay Presentation

Willa Cather's novel *My Antonia* shares the incredible story of American immigration patterns. The characters, especially Jim and Antonia, develop relationships of depth and empathy in their youth but eventually move in their own directions. By leaving Nebraska, Jim abandons the prairie and its hardships; his admiration for Antonia grows in that Jim romanticizes her strengths and diminishes her losses. The further that Jim moves away from the Nebraska prairie, the greater his wealth and education grow, as his life takes him in a cosmopolitan direction. Jim's eastward migration shifts his focus up the ladder of social status even as his thoughts remain with his childhood companions from the Nebraska homesteads. His fear of seeing Antonia old and withered is relieved at the end when he visits her on her farm and sees that her spirit is unbroken. The novel defines the way people interact during the waves of immigration and how deeply and kindly they connect.

The novel's protagonist Jim leaves the Nebraska prairie in a series of steps that separate him from the land. As he separates from the land, he romanticizes it and those associated with it. Jim moves from the farm to Black Hawk, then to Lincoln, then to New York. When Jim arrives on the farm, he is already at a higher status than the Bohemian immigrants because his grandparents homesteaded earlier. When Jim moves to Black Hawk, his status increases again, as it does when he moves to Lincoln, and then to New York. Interestingly, each of Jim's travels eastward increase his social status.

Each of Jim's moves take him up the social ladder and his own hardships decrease, while those on the prairie do not necessarily feel this same level of relief. When Jim leaves the farm for town, his access to fine goods increases as does his associations with people of the merchant and management classes. When Jim moves to Lincoln, he has a greater access to the fine things in life as does Lena whom he dates briefly. Lena's business prospects increase dramatically as she becomes a sought after seamstress of fine clothing. Finally, Jim's final move to New York bring him to one of the world's most cosmopolitan cities. With this move comes his fear of returning to Black Hawk and Antonia, as he does not want to see her broken by poverty and deprivation. He wants to keep a romanticized vision of her life as being carefree and happy.

Jim's romantic vision comes true for him at the end of the story. He and Antonia hold onto the shared incommunicable truth of their mutual past. Jim has envisioned Antonia's life through a romantic lens as though her continued connection with the prairie brought her youthful vivacity. Though at the end, Antonia still displays a strong sense of self and pride in her life because she has not changed much from the youthful rebellious young girl, she has experienced poverty and deprivation that comes with living off the land.

Conclusively, Jim's experience of leaving the prairie for a higher level of civilization is likely similar to many generations of Americans who left the homesteaded farms of the past. The

American homestead movement encouraged settlement by European immigrants and allowed for expanded trade. It also created a romanticized sense of beauty of farm life. Today, like Jim, many readers still long for a romanticized farm life with characters of unbroken spirits. *My Antonia serves* as an excellent tale of the American romantic dream.

Persuasive Letter Example

Persuasive writing is a mainstay in the media industry and has been for centuries. Human beings seem to have an almost inherent desire to convince others into agreement. We write persuasively, read persuasively, and interact persuasively.

All marketing and advertising is persuasive in its nature, because all advertising shares the purpose of convincing a consumer to purchase a product or service. Whether we need it or not, we are bombarded with messages about the variety of things that we supposedly need. Financial advice, dry cleaning, specialty coffee, and baby clothes boutiques all work hard to persuade shoppers to buy from them.

As well, persuasive writing is sometimes used for ill purposes like propaganda and spreading negative ideas. For this reason, readers should be aware of persuasive techniques and able to identify unethical messages so that they can choose what to believe and what to refute.

Many times, persuasive writing can be a force for positive change by helping readers understand why updated policies will create constructive change. People are sometimes reluctant to accept change, and persuasive writing can be used to help in transitions. For example, a community may need to update the flood-prevention measures which requires different expenditures. The local government may use persuasive writing or persuasive speaking measures to communicate to citizens about the necessary improvements.

Since the advent of the Internet, the uses for persuasive writing have increased exponentially. Today, no one can open Facebook or similar sites without running across at least one persuasive posting or comment on social media. Some people have suggested that the lack of in-person interaction has changed the way people communicate online, especially while attempting to be persuasive. Today, persuasive writing is found in advertising, in editorials, in letters, in reviews and commentaries, and on social media.

For our purposes, we will review a persuasive letter to see an example of how persuasive writing works. The letter will be written from a customer's perspective to a restaurant owner to suggest a menu change. People write letters, sometimes in the form of emails, to business on a regular basis. The style of persuasion will use a moderate, professional tone.

Infographic: Persuasive Writing

Persuasive Letter Brainstorm

For this brainstorm, the writer wants to keep the information short, because a letter typically runs 200-400 words. There is not a lot of room for significant depth or detail to support the thesis statement. Letter writers need to keep the writing efficient and concise. The following brainstorm list will cover the topic: a customer making a suggestion to a restaurant owner for a menu change.

Gluten free	Healthier choices	More menu options
Lactose free	Menu unclear	Challenges
Mexican foods	Processed foods	Label the menu

Infographic: Three Column Notes

On Demand Instruction

Three-Column Note Taking

Three-column notes are a great tool for research papers. When you come across a point of interest, write down the source at the top of the page.

Main Ideas	Details	Observations
Ideas Thoughts Page number	Paraphrase the idea	Why does this idea interest you? What is your analysis? What is it related to?

www.OnDemandInstruction.net

Persuasive Brainstorm Analysis

This brainstorm is very short compared to other brainstorms. For the purpose of a letter, the writer would want to compose a brainstorm comprised of just a few details. If there is too much information, then it cannot fit into a one-page letter. So, the brainstorm needs to be brief. This brainstorm includes the basic information that the restaurant menu should be changed to include healthy food choices. Most people would agree that it is a good idea to offer healthy food choices, so the persuasion in this instance should be moderate.

Notice that the details included in this brainstorm all follow the general theme of creating a modern menu—one that is labeled, one with healthier options, and one that recognizes the variety of diets people follow.

Persuasive Letter Planning

Since the letter is going to be limited to such a small amount of space, a complicated plan or graphic organizer is not needed. For a short piece of writing like a letter, a simple plan will suffice. A mind map can work well when a simple plan is needed.

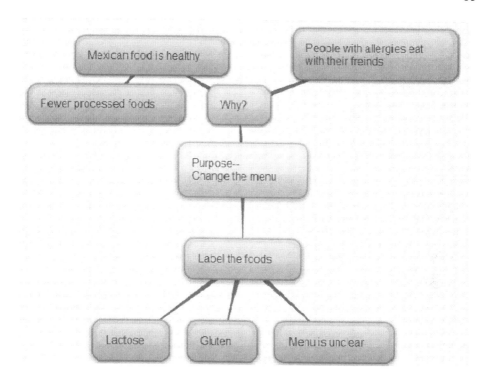

In this mind map, the purpose is noted in the center—change the menu. This is the main point that the letter will get across to the restaurant owner.

The plan includes two subsections under the main topic—*why* and *label the foods*. These subtopics will become the support for the main purpose, to persuade the restaurant owner to change the menu. By explaining to the owner why the menu needs to be changed and by giving specific examples on how to label the menu, the owner will understand what is requested.

As with every piece of writing, the better organized a writer is during the early steps of the writing process, the better organized the final writing will be. Anytime there is an opportunity to brainstorm and plan carefully, take advantage of the occasion. The small amount of time spent organizing can result a smoother writing process and better piece of writing as a result.

Persuasive Letter Rough Draft

Dear Manager:

I visited Jose's Taco Joint last week. It was sad that none of the employees knew what gluten-free or lactose intolerance was and which menu items fit those diets. I have a form of celiac disease that disallows me from eating any gluten, and I happen to be sensitive to dairy too. Both foods make me extremely ill so I am unable to eat them. No one on staff was able to help me choose a meal that would be safe to eat.

Can you imagine going to a restaurant with the fear that you could get food poisoning by half of the foods on the menu? That is what it is like. People with food allergies eat with friends and family in restaurants, just like everyone else. We need to know what foods are safe for us to eat to avoid becoming sick.

Persuasive Editing and Revising

This letter is off to a good start in the rough draft. It includes both the thesis statement, where the menu change is suggested, and the details. The support in this letter includes the explanation as to why labeling menu foods is helpful to people with food allergies. It also includes an explanation of challenges that people with allergies face.

The writer could improve this piece by ending it with specific details on the changes to make. The rough draft ends abruptly rather than ending with a conclusion that details what is needed.

As well, business letter formatting should be used in this letter. That includes:

Block format paragraphs

Sender's address

Recipient's address

Salutation

Persuasive Letter Presentation

Sam Stokes

123 Main St.

Longmont, CO 80501

Jose's Taco Joint

456 Main St.

Longmont, CO 80501

Dear Owner/Manager:

I visited Jose's Taco Joint last week. It was sad that none of the employees knew what gluten-free or lactose intolerance was and which menu items fit those diets. I have a form of celiac disease that disallows me from eating any gluten, and I happen to be sensitive to dairy too. Both foods make me extremely ill so I am unable to eat them. No one on staff was able to help me choose a meal that would be safe to eat. I would appreciate if you would update the menu so that foods are clearly labeled and train the staff on food allergies.

Can you imagine going to a restaurant with the fear that you could get food poisoning by half of the foods on the menu? That is what it is like. People with food allergies eat with friends and family in restaurants, just like everyone else. We need to know what foods are safe for us to eat to avoid becoming sick.

If you would please consider labeling your menu with which foods are gluten free, lactose free, and nut free, people with food allergies could eat at Jose's Taco Joint without concern. Also, informing your staff about food allergies would make the experience much more comfortable. I appreciate you considering this request.

Sincerely,

Sam Stokes

The finalized version of the letter looks more complete. The writer uses business letter formatting by including the missing components from the rough draft. The final version has the sender's address, recipient's address, block paragraphs, and the salutation. Regardless of what style of writing you are working on, use the correct format.

The content is spread across three paragraphs. The first paragraph introduces the thesis statement-I would appreciate if you would update the menu so that foods are clearly labeled and train the staff on food allergies. The second paragraph illustrates the situation clearly.

All three paragraphs are persuasive in that the writer is trying to convince the restaurant owner to make the changes. The writer uses a polite but straightforward tone and sticks to the facts. This makes for strong writing and a convincing letter.

Professional Memo Example

Professional memos are used in nearly every business and organization. They are official documents, where professionals communicate information, establish new policies, request information, or create change. Executives use professional memos to let employees know what is needed from them.

The writing style for a memo is mostly expository, although it may have an element of persuasion to it, especially when asking people to make a change. Change is hard, and changes in policies or practices can be difficult for many people, so being persuaded into making a change can be most effective. Although memos oftentimes include facts, data, or statistics, they do not necessarily include the in-text citations or bibliographic details that research writing would.

Memos use the same format, regardless of who is writing one or what the organization is. Memos predate emails by several decades but use a similar formatting style.

Infographic: Essays in Everyday Use

Professional Memo Format

TO: (Sender's name and position)

FROM: (Recipient's name and position)

DATE: (date of sending)

SUBJECT: (Topic of the memo)

As well, throughout the piece, use block format paragraphs. Use subheadings in emboldened type, and all text is left justified. If there are attachments to the memo, list those on the bottom of the memo page.

For the purposes of this book, we will write a memo to communicate a new procedure for phone etiquette. This memo is being sent from a small business owner to all employees. The problem being addressed is inconsistent phone manners, and the solution is outlined.

Memo Brainstorm

Just like with the persuasive letter, the memo is a short piece of writing. This particular memo will explain a new policy to employees. The style will include some expository and some persuasive writing. Since only one to two pages of content are needed, the brainstorm necessities only few details.

Topic: a new policy is being put into place starting immediately

Problem: people's manners on phone calls are inconsistent

Problem: three clients have complained about the employees' phone manners

Solution: Everyone will use the same phone manners and same phone procedures

Solution: A training is planned for next week to practice these procedures

Memo Brainstorm Analysis

This brainstorm looks different than others that we have seen so far. This brainstorm is much shorter than the others by including only five bullet points. Sometimes, when we are writing about a topic that we know very well, a shorter brainstorm will suffice.

Also notice that this brainstorm includes more in-depth information about each of the listed items. This allows the writer to include information in a grouped manner rather than creating a separate bullet for each idea.

Too, this brainstorm uses labels for each of the ideas. The labels create a level of organization not used in previous brainstorm examples. While brainstorming, if the information is already organized in your mind, go ahead and organize it on paper in the same way. This saves time later in the writing process and allows for the writer to organize and brainstorm simultaneously, which some enjoy doing.

Infographic: Why Organize Your Writing

On Demand Instruction

Why Organize Your Writing?

Writers get one chance to show off their good ideas. Make sure writing is organized so those ideas come across well to the reader.

Organized Writing Is:

1. Easy to read

2. Logical

3. Flows clearly

4. Interesting

5. Engaging

6. What the reader want to learn about

7. Showing off the writer's talent

Organized writing shows the writer's intelligence, expertise on the topic and ability to communicate clearly.

Memo Planning

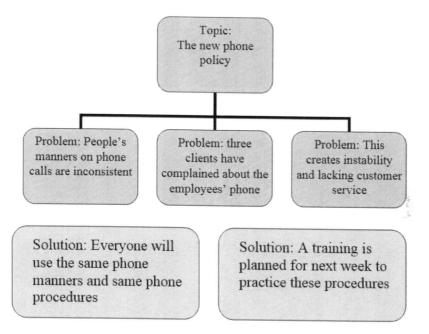

This plan shows a hierarchal structure between the brainstormed information. We see that the topic is the most important element of the plan; it is at the top and is the only topic listed. Visually, the topic dominates the whole graphic organizer as its center point and its focus. The memo's purpose is to address this new phone policy on all its levels.

The next level of the hierarchy includes the problems. In the brainstorm, only two problems were listed, but in the graphic organizer, the problems section was expanded to include three problems. Although the problems are intertwined and depend on each other for their control of the situation, each one should be individually addressed in the memo.

Finally, the two solutions make up the last layer of information in the graphic organizer. The solutions solve the problems and fully address the topic listed for this memo. The solutions will become the conclusion for this piece of writing and will wrap up the information letting employees know what is needed from them.

Memo Drafting

The generational divide has been a topic of conversation for decades, as each generation ages and points out differences in how things used to be. Today, things are no different. In our field, we cater to a wide variety of clientele from every age group and every walk of life. Our small business clients are highly varied but share common communication expectations. Because of concerns that we have received from clientele, we have recognized the problem—inconsistent phone manners have created instability and lacking customer service.

The New Phone Policy

To address the issue of client expectations and communication protocols around phone manners, the new phone policy goes into effect immediately.

Upcoming Training

Next week, Tuesday, March 1, 2016 all staff members will meet at 2pm for the professional development training on this policy.

Memo Editing and Revising

This memo is a good start but needs some work before it will be a solid, final draft.

For starters, the memo is missing the proper memo format, which includes: sender, recipient, date, and subject. Since that is the accepted format, it should be followed on every memo.

In terms of content, one area to improve the memo would be the addition of details on the policy; knowing what the writer is trying to say would be helpful. As well, the indication that age differences makes an unfair assumption about employees and should be replaced with factual information.

Finally, a conclusion does wonders for wrapping up any piece of writing. Anytime there is an opportunity to finish off a piece of writing with a conclusion, take it. The conclusion ends the piece in a clear, clean, concise manner. Too, attaching the new policy would assist the readers so that they can read the new material prior to the meeting, which would make them more efficient.

Memo Presentation

TO: All Staff

FROM: Donald McGovern, Director of Operations

DATE: February 23, 2016

SUBJECT: New Telephone Policy

The fast-paced environment of business makes it challenging for professional to meet every client's needs all the time. In our field, we cater to a wide variety of clientele from every age group and every walk of life. Our small business clients are highly varied but share common communication expectations. Because of concerns that we have received from clientele, we have recognized the problem—inconsistent phone manners have created instability and lacking customer service. In our continued effort to support our clients' needs, it is time to update our telephone communication policy.

The New Phone Policy

To address the issue of client expectations and communication protocols around phone manners, the new phone policy goes into effect immediately.

This new policy includes the topics:

Answering incoming calls

Acknowledging client concerns

Communicating when in a noisy office

Returning calls on time

Conference calls

Leaving voicemails

Upcoming Training

Below is attached the new policy and the procedures related to the training; please review the attachment prior to the scheduled all staff training. Next week, Tuesday, March 1, 2016 all staff members will meet at 2pm for the professional development training on this policy, led by communications coach Susanne D'Angelo.

With more consistent communication practices, we can support each other more easily and serve our clientele more efficiently.

Attachments: New Phone Policy

Research Response Example

This writing example is a short research essay like the kind that a student would write in a secondary or college course. It is customary for instructors to assign short essays that require students to conduct a bit of research during the writing process. These papers can be quite a bit of work for a secondary student but something that a college student creates with ease. In both cases, the expectations are similar.

Expectations for a short research essay include: a strong, clear thesis statement that is the result of the research, well-organized introduction paragraph, in-depth body paragraphs with in-text citations, a conclusion that wraps up the paper, and a works cited page or bibliography that lists the research sources.

For this essay, we are going to conduct research on the question: Who was Amelia Earhart and what did she do. The paper will be an expository research paper with information that answers the research question and informs the reader on the topic. Like other essays, research papers can be written to persuade, enlighten, educate, compare/contrast, or for other reasons. The most common form of research paper is the expository, which will explain a topic without persuading. Its only purpose is to share factual information. Because of this, an expository research essay uses an expository thesis statement, one that will explain in a clear and calm manner to the reader.

There are several different research formats that could be used to layout a research paper. Modern Language Association (MLA) is the format used in most English/Language Arts courses. Associated Press (AP) is used in Journalism and publishing. American Psychological Association (APA) is used in Psychology and Social Sciences. And there is a variety of other formats used for research papers. Anytime you are asked to write a research paper or project, be sure to ask what format is expected and follow that format exactly.

Infographic: Research Process

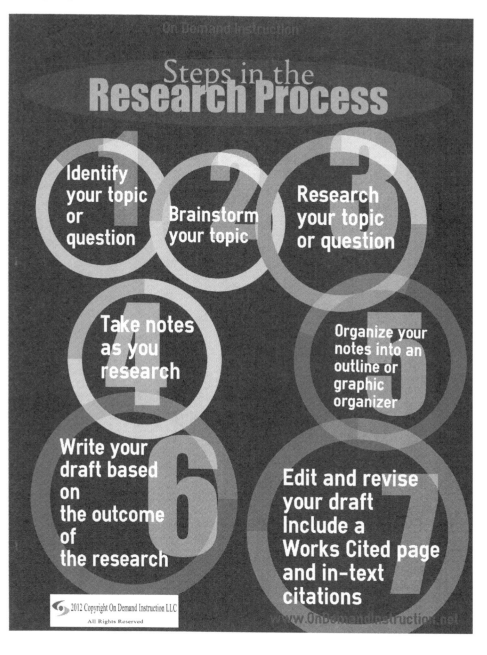

Research Brainstorm

For the research paper brainstorm, we will use a bulleted list of ideas, questions, researched facts, and information on the topic. You can include the URLS and other identifying notes on the research sources you read along the way.

Who was Amelia Earhart?

What did Earhart accomplish?

What is Earhart known for?

What was her childhood, background, and social environment like?

What training and education did she have?

Did she get encouragement or criticism or both?

http://www.ameliaearhart.com/about/bio.html

Childhood: outdoorsy girl, loved sledding, hunting, and climbing trees.

Kept a scrapbook of information about successful women in male-oriented roles.

Education: Hyde Park HS 1915 IL, Ogonta (Philadelphia finishing school), Columbia, NY (one year 1919, one year 1924 left because of lacking funds)

http://www.notablebiographies.com/Du-Fi/Earhart-Amelia.html

Lived with her wealthy grandparents in Atcheson, KS until age 12.

Saw her first plane at a state fair in Des Moines but was not impressed.

Father was an alcoholic. Its effect—she disliked alcohol and desired financial security. Her mother eventually left him to live with friends in IL.

Work experience—nurse during WWI in Toronto. Its effect—she was a lifelong pacifist.

First flight—1920. Shortly after—took lessons, got her flight license, bought her own plane, but couldn't afford to continue the hobby.

http://www.ameliaearhart.com/about/bio.html

In 1928, flew the plane *Friendship* from Newfoundland to Wales in the first cross-Atlantic flight flown by a woman. Three previous pilots were killed in their attempts. The effect—world-wide recognition, ticker-tape parade in NYC, reception at the White House, rest of her life dedicated to flying.

1931 married to publisher George Putnam in what she called a "partnership" with "dual control", so basically a modern marriage.

Accomplishments

http://www.ameliaearhart.com/about/achievements.html

10/22/1922 Broke women's altitude record

6/18/1928 First woman to fly across the Atlantic

Fall 1928 published book *20 Hours 40 Minutes*

Fall 1928 became aviation editor at Cosmopolitan Magazine

6/30/1930 Set women's speed record

7/5/1930 Set speed record

8/8/1931 Set women's autogiro altitude record

5/21/1932 First woman to fly solo over Atlantic (for this awarded National Geographic Society's gold medal from President Herbert Hoover; Congress awarded her the Distinguished Flying Cross; she wrote book *The Fun of It* about her journey)

8/25/1932 first woman to fly solo nonstop coast to coast; set women's nonstop transcontinental speed record

Fall 1932 elected president of The Ninety Nines, a women's aviation club

7/8/1933 broke her own transcontinental speed record

1/11/1935 first person to solo fly across Pacific; first flight where a civilian aircraft carried a two-way radio

4/20/1935 First person to fly solo from LA to Mexico City

6/1/1937 began flight around the world; first person to fly from the Red Sea to India

Infographic: Why Take Notes

On Demand Instruction

WHY TAKE NOTES?

Simply hearing something sometimes isn't enough to remember it, which is why note taking is so important. Notes capture information for later use.

Taking notes in CLASS

Keep organized and neat so you can use your notes later.

Start on a fresh piece of paper every time you sit down to take notes. Write the date at the top and any identifying information (lecturer, class, subject, etc.).

Don't try to write everything down; just work on getting the main ideas.

Leave space in case you need to add something in later.

Read over your notes as soon after class as you can. Fill in anything that you don't understand or can't read.

Common Abbreviations and Symbols

cf (compare)

i.e. (that is)

e.g. (for example)

w/ (with)

w/o (without)

&, + (and)

= (equals, is)

Taking notes from TEXTBOOKS

Organize your notes the same as you would in class.

Write down the name of the book and the chapter or section.

Leave space in the margin for your own notes or comments.

Keep your textbook notes separate from your class notes.

Get a general idea of what the reading is about.

Go back over the material, reading it carefully. Look for main ideas.

Don't copy the information directly; write in your own words. It will help you remember the information better.

Summarize the main ideas at the end and circle them.

www.OnDemandInstruction.net

Research Planning

In the planning step, the writer takes the information from the brainstorm and organizes it into a coherent, organized pattern. Using a graphic organizer like a plan, outline, or three-column notes format can make this task easier. With the plan, he writer can use the organizer to create the rough draft. At this step, being highly organized is very important. Always use a graphic organizer that suits your personal style and your thought processes. Once you have a graphic organizer that you like, then continue using it for other papers and projects. If it works, stick with it. For this research paper, we will use a bulleted list.

Since a research paper requires a writer to conduct research as well as to cite the sources used, writers need to keep track of what information is used in different parts of the paper. For MLA format, the research is noted in two places: the in-text citation that comes at the end of each sentence that includes information from research and in the Works Cited page which is a list of all sources at the very end of the paper. Be sure to connect the research with the information in both citations and entries to keep organized.

Research Paper Bulleted Organized List

Introduction

Hook with an Earhart Quote: "After midnight, the moon set, and I was alone with the stars. I have often said that the lure of flying is the lure of beauty, and I need no other flight to convince me that the reason flyers fly, whether they know it or not, is the esthetic appeal of flying."

Thesis Statement: Amelia Earhart is well known as one of the first accomplished female pilots, but her accomplishments include breaking men's records and attempting feats that no pilots (male or female) had done before.

- Who was Amelia Earhart?
- What did Earhart accomplish?
- What is Earhart known for?
- What was her childhood, background, and social environment like?
- What training and education did she have?
- Did she get encouragement or criticism or both?

Body Paragraph 1-Childhood

Source: http://www.ameliaearhart.com/about/bio.html

- Childhood: outdoorsy girl, loved sledding, hunting, and climbing trees.

- Kept a scrapbook of information about successful women in male-oriented roles.

- Education: Hyde Park HS 1915 IL, Ogonta (Philadelphia finishing school), Columbia, NY (one year 1919, one year 1924 left because of lacking funds)

Source: http://www.notablebiographies.com/Du-Fi/Earhart-Amelia.html

- Lived with her wealthy grandparents in Atcheson, KS until age 12.

Father was an alcoholic. Its effect—she disliked alcohol and desired financial security. Her mother eventually left him to live with friends in IL.

Body Paragraph 2-Introduction to Flight

Source: http://www.notablebiographies.com/Du-Fi/Earhart-Amelia.html

- Saw her first plane at a state fair in Des Moines but was not impressed.

• First flight—1920. Shortly after—took lessons, got her flight license, bought her own plane, but couldn't afford to continue the hobby.

Body Paragraph 3-Earhart's accomplishments

Source: http://www.ameliaearhart.com/about/bio.html

• In 1928, flew the plane *Friendship* from Newfoundland to Wales in the first cross-Atlantic flight flown by a woman. Three previous pilots were killed in their attempts. The effect—world-wide recognition, ticker-tape parade in NYC, reception at the White House, rest of her life dedicated to flying.

Accomplishments

Source:

http://www.ameliaearhart.com/about/achievements.html

Broke altitude records 1922, 1931

Speed records 1930, 1933

6/18/1928 First woman to fly across the Atlantic

Publishing: 20 Hours 40 Minutes, aviation editor at

5/21/1932 First woman to fly solo over Atlantic (for this awarded National geographic Society's gold medal from President Herbert Hoover; Congress awarded her the

Distinguished Flying Cross; wrote book The Fun of It about her journey)

8/25/1932 first woman to fly solo nonstop coast to coast; set women's nonstop transcontinental speed record

Fall 1932 elected president of The Ninety Nines, a women's aviation club

1/11/1935 first person to solo fly across Pacific; first flight where a civilian aircraft carried a two-way radio

6/1/1937 began flight around the world; first person to fly from the Red Sea to India

Conclusion-Earhart's Legacy

Work experience—nurse during WWI in Toronto. Its effect—she was a lifelong pacifist.

1931 married to publisher George Putnam in what she called a "partnership" with "dual control", so basically a modern marriage.

Quotes:

"...decide...whether or not the goal is worth the risks involved. If it is, stop worrying...."

"The most difficult thing is the decision to act. The rest is merely tenacity. The fears are paper tigers. You can do anything you decide to do. You can act to change and control your life and the procedure. The process is its own reward."

Sources:

www.ameliaearhart.com

http://www.notablebiographies.com/Du-Fi/Earhart-Amelia.html

Infographic: Research Writing

On Demand Instruction
WHAT IS A RESEARCH PAPER?

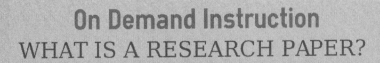

A research paper is an essay
that takes factual research,
which was borrowed from expert sources,
to support a thesis statement.

All research is documented, using a particular
research guideline (MLA, APA, Turabian, Chicago)

Strong
thesis
statement

Include these in
every research
paper

Thesis support
must come
from research

In-text source
citations in
all body
paragraphs for
each instance of
borrowed data

Works Cited
page created
in MLA format

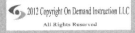

www.ondemandinstruction.net

Research Drafting

Amelia Earhart is well known one of the first accomplished female pilots, but her endeavors included breaking men's records and attempting feats that no pilots had done before. Her accomplishments include setting speed and altitude records, solo flights, and first flights as an early aviatrix. Earhart is known as one of the most inspiring groundbreaking women in American history, as her accomplishments have inspired millions of people since her untimely death.

Amelia Earhart lived with her grandparents in Atcheson, Kansas. She kept a scrapbook of successful women in male-oriented roles and (Biography). Earhart and her family suffered the effects of her father's alcoholism and moved often due to the financial and personal hardships caused by his addiction (Biography). Earhart's education was moderate for the time period. She enjoyed the benefit of some college and was able to travel to Canada to volunteer during the war as a nurse.

Earhart's experience with airplanes started off slow but picked up as her resources improved. The first time she saw an airplane at the state fair in Des Moines, she was not impressed (Amelia Earhart Biography). But once she took her first flight, aviation was in her blood. Earhart took lessons, earned her pilot's license, and bought her first airplane by working multiple part time jobs (Amelia Earhart Biography). Although the hobby was expensive, Earhart did not let that slow her down, she kept herself open to flying possibilities that came later.

Her first big flight was the Atlantic crossing in 1928, which won her international recognition, a ticker-tape parade, and a visit to the White House (Biography). Earhart's accomplishments include setting and breaking flight records for speed and altitude. As well, she broke records and set firsts as a female pilot and as any pilot, as many of her acknowledgements were for male and female pilots (Biography). Earhart wrote about her experiences, edited for Cosmopolitan Magazine, and headed up the Ninety-Nines women's aviation club (Achievements).

Amelia Earhart's legacy is one of courage, resolve, and persistence; she said people must decide, "whether or not the goal is worth the risks involved. If it is, stop worrying". Hers is the story of a modern woman who sets out to accomplish her goals and did just that. Her volunteer experience during WWI made her a life-long pacifist. She was an intelligent, competent, and self-driven pilot who happened to inspire all of America with her determination.

Research Editing and Revising

This rough draft is a good start and has the basic information readers want to see in a research essay. What would make it better would be a strong hook statement to start off the essay, perhaps a quote from Amelia Earhart herself. Some of the paragraphs seem to be missing either introduction or conclusion sentences, so verifying that every paragraph begins well and ends well could improve the essay. The conclusion is a bit dull and could be improved in its tone and style to energize the reader about this topic. Also, the Works Cited page, which should list all of the research sources, should be the last page of the essay.

Infographic: Correct the Errors

On Demand Instruction

CORRECT THE ERRORS

What are Conventions & Mechanics?

These include all the little details that make the writing correct. Sometimes, people think that the ideas or messages are the only things that matter in writing.

Have you ever tried to say something but just could not get it to come out right? Even though your ideas may have been wonderful, the way they were presented was filled with errors so the message did not come across. Without conventions, you will have a difficult time getting your message to your audience.

Capitalization
First words, proper nouns, titles, etc.

Spelling
All words are spelled correctly.

Punctuation
Periods, quotation marks, commas, question marks, exclamation points, dashes, slashes, parentheses, colons, apostrophes, etc.

Sentences
Structure is sound and sentences make sense.

Paragraphing
Writing is organized and ideas follow each other.

Grammar/Usage
Words and ideas are used correctly and make sense.

By using corrected writing, a writer can:

- Get their point across efficiently
- Change the reader's mind about a topic
- Share thoughts in a way that means something

If a writer's ideas are presented in a mess of errors, the reader will hold no interest due to the distractions.

www.ondemandinstruction.net

Research Presentation

"After midnight, the moon set, and I was alone with the stars. I have often said that the lure of flying is the lure of beauty, and I need no other flight to convince me that the reason flyers fly, whether they know it or not, is the esthetic appeal of flying." Amelia Earhart is well known one of the first accomplished female pilots, but her accomplishments included breaking men's records and attempting feats that no pilots (male or female) had done before. Her accomplishments include setting speed and altitude records, solo flights, and first flights as an early aviatrix. Earhart is known as one of the most inspirational groundbreaking women in American history, as her accomplishments have inspired millions of people since her untimely death.

Amelia Earhart lived with her grandparents in Atcheson, Kansas. She was known for hunting with a rifle, wild sledding, and tree climbing, eschewing the fancy dresses in preference for comfortable, practical clothing (Biography). She kept a scrapbook of successful women in male-oriented roles (Biography). Earhart and her family suffered the effects of her father's alcoholism and moved often due to the financial and personal hardships caused by his addiction (Biography). Earhart's education was moderate for the time period. She enjoyed the benefit of some college and was able to travel to Canada to volunteer during the war as a nurse. The freedom that Earhart experienced as a child likely added to her confident spirit to follow her dreams.

Earhart's experience with airplanes started off slow but picked up as her resources improved. The first time she saw an airplane at the state fair in Des Moines, she was not impressed (Amelia Earhart Biography). But once she took her first flight, aviation was in her blood. Earhart took lessons, earned her pilot's license, and bought her first airplane by working multiple part time jobs (Amelia Earhart Biography). Although the hobby was expensive, Earhart did not let that slow her down, she kept herself open to flying possibilities that came later.

Once Earhart was able to organize the resources to support her career, things took off for her. Her first big flight was the Atlantic crossing in 1928, which won her international recognition, a ticker-tape parade, and a visit to the White House (Biography). Earhart's accomplishments include setting and breaking flight records for speed and altitude. As well, she broke records and set firsts as a female pilot and as any pilot, as many of her acknowledgements were for male and female pilots (Biography). Earhart wrote about her experiences, edited for Cosmopolitan Magazine, and headed up the Ninety-Nines women's aviation club (Achievements). As a dearly loved and well acknowledged pilot, Earhart's death while attempting an around-the-world flight was one of the tragedies of the time; her loss was a loss for all Americans.

Amelia Earhart's legacy is one of courage, resolve, and persistence; she said people must decide, "whether or not the goal is worth the risks involved. If it is, stop worrying". Hers is the story of a modern woman who sets out to accomplish her goals and did just that. Her marriage was a "partnership" with "dual control", so a modern marriage of equality. Her volunteer experience during WWI made her a life-long pacifist. She was an intelligent, competent, and self-driven pilot who happened to inspire all of America with her determination. The effect that Earhart left on us in her own words, "The most difficult thing is the decision to act. The rest is merely tenacity. The fears are paper tigers. You can do anything you decide to do. You can act to change and control your life and the procedure. The process is its own reward."

Works Cited

Biography. Amelia Earhart: The Official Website. N.d. Web.

22 March 2016.

Achievements. Amelia Earhart: The Official Website. N.d.

Web. 22 March 2016.

Amelia Earhart Biography. Encyclopedia or World Biography.

Notable Biographies. N.d. Web. 22 March 2016.

Narrative Essay Example

The narrative is an appealing writing style. From our very first days, human beings hang onto narratives like they are our lifelines. We listen to the stories that our parents tell at home, we watch stories on television, and we read stories in books. From narratives, we learn about history, science, and literature. Whole cultures depend upon narratives to preserve their social values.

Today, we love narratives as much as any other society. Ask anyone what their favorite stories are and most people will answer with a television show, a fictional book, a religious text, or a podcast that motivates them. We love narratives both in reading them and writing them.

For the purpose of this task, we will examine the writing process for a narrative around the topic: the time I got lost. For this narrative, we are taking the perspective of a young person, a child. For anyone, getting lost can be a frightening experience, but for a child, it can be particularly dangerous, even terrifying.

Infographic: Narrative Writing

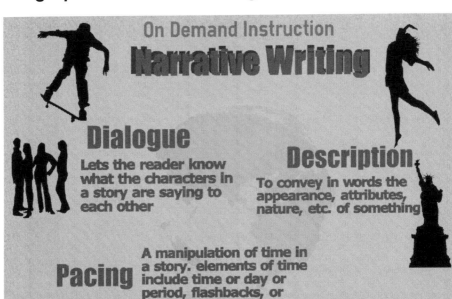

On Demand Instruction

Narrative Writing

Dialogue
Lets the reader know what the characters in a story are saying to each other

Description
To convey in words the appearance, attributes, nature, etc. of something

Pacing
A manipulation of time in a story. elements of time include time or day or period, flashbacks, or foreshadowing.

What is a Narrative?
When you are writing a narrative essay, think of it as telling a story. These essays can be based on personal events. This lets you express yourself as creatively as you'd like.

Write a clear introduction that sets the tone for the rest of the essay. Don't leave the reader guessing about the purpose of your writing.

Remember, you are in control of your essay, so take it where you want it to go! (Just make sure your readers can follow your lead.)

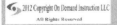

www.ondemandinstruction.net

Narrative Brainstorm

Some people have to touch things to understand them. If you have ever been a person who learns by doing, working with your hands, or moving your body to learn, you may be a kinesthetic learner. These are people who become the mechanics, ballerinas, and soccer stars of the world. They learn by moving.

These people tend to enjoy being able to move objects around during their brainstorming and organizing process as well. For them, the ability to move their ideas physically helps them to process information and problem solve.

To demonstrate how to brainstorm and plan for these learners, we will use sticky notes to brainstorm and plan this narrative.

The day I got lost at the zoo	Gorillas Elephants Lions Monkeys	Ran to play hide and go seek
No one was around. Very scary	Mom told me, "Always stay where you can see me."	Moms always seem to know best

In the image, we used sticky notes so that each note would hold one idea from the young writer. A young person may brainstorm fewer ideas overall for a story than an older writer, so six ideas in the brainstorm may be plenty. Kinesthetic learners can benefit from using sticky notes or notecards because they can be shifted around to fit any pattern or organization.

The day I got
lost at the zoo

Mom told me,
"Always stay
where you can
see me."

Gorillas
Elephants
Lions
Monkeys

Ran to play
hide and go
seek

No one was
around.
Very scary

Moms always
seem to know
best

Narrative Planning

Notice that this plan is a restructured version of the brainstorm. If these were physical sticky notes, the writer could move them around for the best organization. This process is fun and appealing to kinesthetic learners because they have the chance to use their hands and move while learning. This can increase their enjoyment with the writing process and help them to write more.

Infographic: Narrative Writing

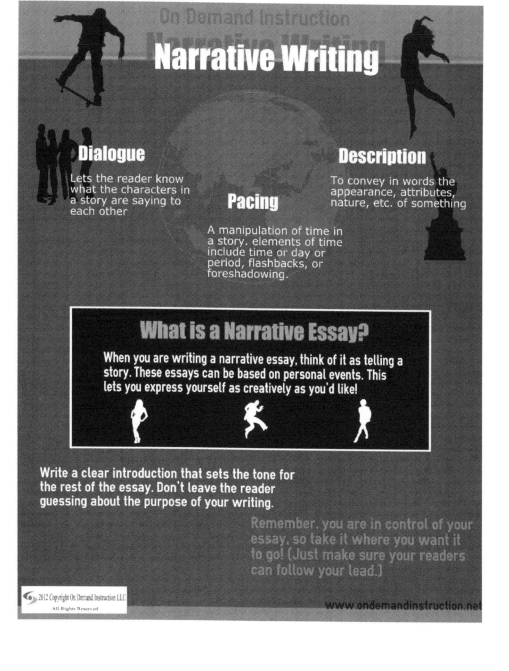

Narrative Drafting

I liked to play funny games with the animals at the zoo. Once I started walking around the zoo on my own, I played hide and seek with the animals. My mom would say, "Always stay where you can see me."

I would hide from the gorillas, elephants, and lions. But the monkeys were always my favorites.

One day, I was playing hide and seek with the monkeys but there was nowhere good to hide, so I started looking for a good place. I found a good spot behind a bench and sat there for a long time. When I stood up, no one was around, and it was very scary.

I ran out from behind the bench, but I couldn't remember which way my mom was. So, I ran as fast as I could. I looked everywhere for my mom, and when I could not find her, I started to cry.

So, there I was running and crying and about three years old. A zoo keeper came up to me and asked if I was lost, and I said yes.

The zoo keeper walked with me to the front of the zoo and there was my mom. She was also crying.

She hugged me so tight that I couldn't breathe. Then she kissed me all over my face. I wasn't crying anymore.

I guess that moms always know best when they say, "Always stay where you can see me." I understood why she said that after I got lost.

Narrative Editing and Revising

In this piece, we have a basic narrative of a child who gets lost at the zoo while playing a game. The story begins with foreshadowing where the mother warns the child to stay close by. Later on, the child gets lost and does not know what to do to solve the problem.

This narrative is a good start in that it has a complete story, is engaging to a wide audience, and is a personal story. This narrative has elements that appeal to many people.

This narrative could be improved with a more extensive introduction. The one here jumps straight into the action without much background information.

Dialogue would also illuminate details about the characters and how they interact. Most people know that small children enjoy playing games, but showing off some details about this character would make an improvement. With a narrative essay, highlighting the lesson learned, or the purpose the paper, is always a good idea.

Narrative Presentation

Ever since I was a little kid, my favorite place to visit was the zoo. My mom used to take me to the zoo to see the animals. Anytime the weather was good, we would be at the zoo visiting. Even though it was my favorite place to visit, one day it became the scariest when I got lost.

One of my favorite things to do was to growl at the animals. My mom would push my stroller up close to the cages so that I could see. I liked to try and talk in their language, so I would growl at them. It seemed like they liked it if someone could speak their language.

Another game I liked to play was hide and seek. I would pull down the hood on my jacket so that the elephants could not see my face. Then I would pop it up and shout, "Surprise! Here I am." I think they liked that game too.

Once I started walking around the zoo on my own, I played hide and seek with the animals. My mom would say, "Always stay where you can see me."

I would hide from the gorillas, elephants, and lions. The monkeys were always my favorites.

One day, I was playing hide and seek with the monkeys but there was nowhere good to hide, so I started looking for a quiet place. I found a good spot behind a bench and sat there for a long time. When I stood up, no one was around, and it was very scary.

I ran out from behind the bench, but I couldn't remember which way my mom was. So, I ran as fast as I could. I looked everywhere for my mom, and when I could not find her, I started to cry.

So, there I was running and crying and about three years old. A zoo keeper came up to me and asked, "Are you lost?"

"Yes, I lost my mom," I said.

"Well, I just got a call that your mom is looking for you. Are you Samuel?" The zoo keeper asked.

"Yes! I am Samuel. Do you know where my mom is?" I asked.

"I sure do. Follow me," said the zoo keeper.

The zoo keeper walked with me to the front of the zoo and there was my mom. She was also crying.

She hugged me so tight that I couldn't breathe. Then she kissed me all over my face. I wasn't crying anymore.

I guess that moms always know best when they say, "Always stay where you can see me." I understood why she said that after I got lost.

Conclusion

Using the writing process will help you to write in an organized and clear manner. Once you have followed the steps on different projects, they will come more naturally until you use them without thinking about it. Over time, as you write for school, work, and personal needs, the steps become more fluid; with each new piece of writing the process becomes quicker. Eventually, you can use the writing process for anything—a speech, a marketing campaign, a work meeting, a professional discussion, a film script, a resume, or any other piece of writing or project you may be creating. The process is a simple, logical one and can suit any need.

The writing process will save a lot of time and help you communicate your thoughts easily. Regardless if you are composing a short answer or an extended research paper, the writing process can guide you through the task.

Writers who use the writing process tend to write more efficiently, effectively, and exactly. Their writing comes across stronger and more professional than writers who write off the cuff. As you work through this process, adjust it to fit your particular needs so that it suits your learning and writing styles.

Infographic: The Writing Process Steps

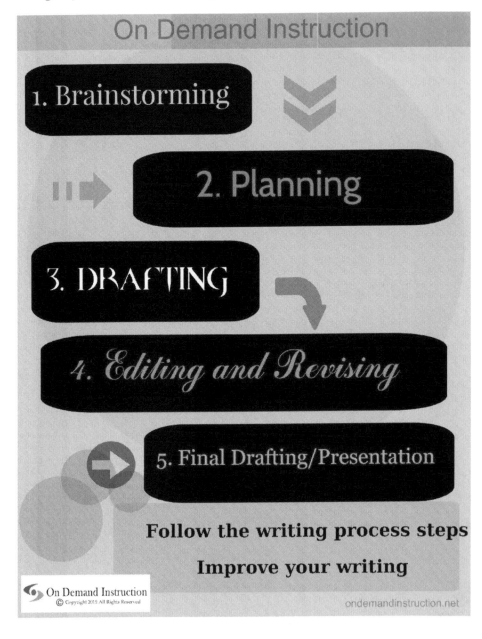

Terms Glossary

Catch (or Hook): This is a statistic, question, or interesting fact that is used to catch the reader's attention at the beginning of a piece of writing.

Topic Statement: This is a sentence used at the beginning of a paragraph that tells what is being proven or shown in that paragraph.

Thesis Statement: This is a sentence used in an essay and tells what is being proven by the essay.

Support Statement: These are statements (reasons, details, facts, etc) that prove that the topic or thesis is true.

Data Statement: These are statements that offer very specific information on the supporting statements to prove that they are true.

Conclusion Statement: This is the last sentence of a paragraph that summarizes what was communicated in the paragraph; it also transitions the ideas from one paragraph to the next.

Transition: This refers to either a word, phrase, or a sentence that shows change in writing (such as one idea to another).

Short Answer (or Short Response): One to four paragraphs that answer a prompt.

Essay: Several paragraphs that prove the thesis statement is true.

Report: A paper that communicates facts; it does not prove a thesis statement.

Persuasive: Writing that attempts to convince the reader to agree with the writer's proposals.

Expository: Writing that teaches the reader about some topic.

Narrative: Writing that tells a story; it is not open-ended but has a purpose to communicate.

Paper: A general term for any piece of writing—short answer, essay, research paper, professional paper, narrative, etc.

Introduction Paragraph: This is the first paragraph of a paper. It includes the topic, thesis statement, and major support.

Body Paragraph: These are the paragraphs between the introduction and conclusion paragraphs. They contain the research, support, details, examples, statistics, and quotations that back up the thesis statement.

Conclusion Paragraph: This is the final paragraph of the paper that summarizes its major points.

Afterward

The purpose of The Simple Guide to The Writing Process is to Help writers improve their writing skills. In this book, we covered what the writing process is and different ways to use it. We also covered how different writers apply the writing process and different tricks for appealing to a variety of writing styles. Five full-length examples were given to illustrate how to apply the writing process for both academic and professional style writing.

Good writers are just people who spent a little more time dedicated to the practice of writing. Like any skill, writing requires that we give it time, energy, and training to succeed. By starting out constructing strong paragraphs, anyone can work into short answers, letters, essays, and research projects and be proficient writers in no time.

Sincerely, we hope that after reading this book that your confidence in writing and using the writing process has improved. Writing is a lifelong process and no one is born a perfect writer. It is a skill that requires practice and ongoing improvement to master.

Check out my author website at:
http://patriciamartinauthor.com

Look for updates and giveaways from On Demand Instruction's full line of books and courses at:
http://ondemandinstruction.com

About the Author—Patricia Martin, MA, MEd

Having spent the last two decades in school, both as a professional student and as an educator, my passion for education and learning is boundless. After many years of studying, I hold undergrad degrees in Literature and History and Master's degrees in Writing and Communication, Educational Leadership, and a Master's Certificate in Creative Writing.

Over the last two decades, I have spent the majority of my time helping people to write better. Sometimes writing better has more to do with feeling more confident and capable than anything else. So many people, kids and adults alike, get the idea that they lack the gift for writing, and they give up. Spending a little more time with these people to prop them up and teach them some tricks has made my career a joy.

Most of my writing is instructional nonfiction and curricular content to support novice readers and writers. I absolutely love creating courses and thrive off of hearing that I was able to help someone work through a challenging situation and return to the creative path.

Writing poetry and novels is a pursuit I share with my family. When my kids were little, I wrote each of them a book series around characters they invented. As they grew, I wrote books to fit their changing interests. My daughter once asked me to write about a character named Lily, who as my daughter described, "Wore a yellow dress, beat up the bad guys, and flew a rocket in space." I happily complied.

Besides teaching and writing, my other love is nature. I love Nordic skiing and snowshoeing in the winter and make a point to get outdoors even on the really cold days. In the summer, I am either lakeside getting ready for kayaking or hitting the road to go camping. Nature is my church, my therapy, my happy place.

Made in the USA
Lexington, KY
10 December 2017